Myths of a Different Feather

Jane Langford
Illustrated by
Paula Zinngrabe Wendland

A Harcourt Achieve Imprint

www.Rigby.com
1-800-531-5015

Literacy by Design Leveled Readers: *Myths of a Different Feather*

ISBN-13:   978-1-4189-3925-0
ISBN-10:   1-4189-3925-0

© 2008 Harcourt Achieve Inc.

Rigby is a trademark of Harcourt Achieve Inc.

Printed in China
1A 2 3 4 5 6 7 8 985 13 12 11 10 09 08 07

Contents

1
The King of the Sky: A Celtic Myth

The Eagle and the Wren

One unquestioned animal ruler governed the creatures roaming the land—the mighty bear, chief of all the beasts of the mountains and plains, who paced around his enormous kingdom bellowing orders to his loyal subjects. In the ocean, the mighty whale ruled the waves, her shrill voice echoing through the bottomless deep. In the world of men and women, there were many leaders, such as kings and queens, emperors and empresses, who sat upon their royal thrones and spoke solemn words. But in all the vast sky that covered the mountains and plains, arched above the oceans, and surrounded the world of men and women, no single creature could claim that he or she ruled all others.

The owl became concerned about the lack of a ruler of the sky, so he called a council, sending messengers to every part of the globe to fetch birds from the North, South, East, and West to attend this meeting of ruffled feathers.

When all the birds were assembled, the owl spoke to them gravely. "My fellow birds, you each know why we are gathered here today."

The doves cooed softly at him, "We dooooo, we dooooo!"

The owl turned his head and flashed his huge orange eyes at the gentle doves, who fell into an uncomfortable silence, tucked their white wings tightly to their sides, and stepped backwards.

Clearing his throat, the owl said sternly, "We are here because we have no leader, and this is a matter of great importance to all of us. Whoooo will lead us in time of trouble, and whoooo will speak for us when wise words need to be spoken?"

"Yooooou are wise!" cooed the doves. "You coo-coo-could rule us!"

The owl closed his golden eyes and shook his head quite slowly, saying, "Nooo, not I."

"Why not?" asked the crow.

The owl opened his eyes again, piercing the crow with his gaze, and said, "I may be something of a sky chief at night, in the silent darkness, but I cannot be king of the sky in the full light of the sun."

The assembly of birds twittered and squawked, shifting restlessly in the nearby branches and on the woodland floor.

"Then whoooo?" cooed the doves.

"Yes, who?" squawked the crow.

"That is what we are here to determine," said the owl. "Therefore, we must organize a competition to choose our leader."

"I hope it will be a fair competition," piped the tiny wren, "since I am so very small."

The owl snapped his head around, fixed his stare on the little wren, and said, "Size and strength are not the only things that matter. Cleverness and intelligence are important, too."

The birds noisily debated the nature of the competition to be held.

"I think the tallest bird should be king," said the heron, stretching her legs and long neck as high as she could. "Or rather, queen."

"No, no," said the turkey, opening his handsome fan. "The bird with the most beautiful tail feathers should rule!"

"Surely the bird with the most beautiful voice would make the best king," said the mockingbird, and he sang a sweet melody to make his point.

"Silence, all of yoooooooou," said the owl. "None of these ideas is acceptable, so I will decide!"

The birds stopped their chatter and listened intently as the owl said grandly, "My fine feathered friends, I have determined that our leader—our king— should be the bird that can fly the highest!"

"Fly the highest, the highest, the highest . . . " echoed all the birds in a single, chirping voice. They craned their necks and looked upward at the vast blue arch of sky above their heads.

The wren saw the towering trees that stretched up into the blue distance and asked, "Would the bird have to fly as high as the tallest trees?"

"Higher," the owl answered.

"Would . . . ," the wren began, swallowing a lump in his throat, "would he need to fly as high as the highest mountain peak?"

The owl leaned forward and stared at the tiny wren. "Higher," the owl said, and several birds, feeling a little uncomfortable, began to back away.

The wren noticed a soft, white pillow of cloud drifting in the brilliant blue. He asked, "Would he have to fly as high as the clouds?"

"Higher still, if he wanted to be king," the owl responded. He leaned back, satisfied that he had frightened all of the questions out of the curious little bird.

Evening closed in, and the birds began to settle down for the night. Some roosted in trees. Some nestled into fields. They all slept soundly—all, that is, except for the wren, whose clever mind would not rest.

The next morning, as the sun climbed above the horizon, the owl beamed approvingly when he saw that all the birds were gathering in the branches of his ancient oak.

He solemnly plucked a soft, white feather from his broad chest and held it up in his sharp talons. "When this feather falls," he announced, "the competition will begin. The rules are simple—each bird must fly from this tree to the very edge of the sky, and the bird whoooo flies highest will be our king!"

As the wren looked around him, he saw the swallow getting set to speed off like an arrow. He spotted the swan flapping in readiness for take-off. And there was the hawk, posed silently, preparing to gracefully glide away. There were more birds than the wren had ever seen before in his life, and he thought, "How can I possibly win against so many?"

Then, from the corner of his eye, he spied the eagle, the mightiest bird of all, holding on to a nearby branch with a powerful grip. The eagle in turn stared hungrily at the wren. A single beat of the eagle's wing could blow the wren off his own perch. A single stab of even one talon could pierce the wren's tiny heart. And a single strike from the eagle's hooked beak would break the poor wren in two.

The wren trembled at the eagle's gaze. The owl saw his fear, and he hooted to the eagle, "Remember, we are here to fly, not to feast. Now, birds, reach for the sky as brothers and sisters, and come back to Earth prepared to serve your new king!"

The white feather dropped from the owl's talons, and WHOOSH, the flurry of wings was deafening. It was like a whirlwind launching itself up into the deep blue sky.

The owl watched intently as the brave birds swept ever higher, calling out, "Good luck to yoooou! May the best bird win!"

The gentle doves echoed his cry. "Good luck to yoooou, coo, coo!"

Like a swirling cloud of smoke, the mass of winged creatures spun higher and higher, and a chorus of twitters, cackles, and calls rose from the ground as the onlookers squawked encouragement to their friends.

After a swift ascent, the flock of birds began to separate. Some birds quickly tired, so they leveled off to try to catch their breath before continuing upward. Others streamed ahead like shooting stars.

The birds looked as if they were trying to catch the sun as it rose higher and higher into the bright morning sky. From the ground they appeared to be nothing more than tiny black specks against the world's wide blue ceiling. But the effort became too much for many of the birds, and one by one, the exhausted creatures flew back to Earth.

The owl shaded his great eyes with one wing and scanned the skies to see who remained in the air. He flew to the height of the tallest tree to get a better look. The eagle was still there, soaring almost effortlessly with great sweeps up into the blue, but as far as the owl could see, all of the other birds were far, far below. "The eagle will be king," thought the owl. "He will be a strong leader."

But just as the owl opened his beak to declare the eagle the victor, a small, dark shape fluttered out from behind the eagle's proud head.

It was the wren! He had hitched a ride on the powerful eagle's back, and here he was, at the last moment, launching himself even higher than his frightening host. The owl watched as the wren flew above the eagle's head, chirping and singing as he rose even higher. "I am king! I am king of the sky!" he called.

Indeed he was king, for the eagle had reached the limit of his strength. He was tired beyond measure, and he did not have the strength to follow the fresh and nimble wren. As the mighty bird tilted the tips of his wings and began to circle downward in defeat, the little wren sang his song of triumph and let it echo across the sky.

"It shall be as I said," the owl declared, smiling up at the joyful wren. "Size is not the only thing that matters—cleverness and intelligence are just as important."

The Wren's Story

In spring and summer, you may see me as I perch happily in the lower branches of a tree, flit to a bush, hop around on the ground in search of seeds and insects, and then flutter back onto a lower limb. You will never see me far from the ground. Only my voice—my trembling song—flies high into the sky and toward the distant clouds. Long ago I flew there too, into the highest reaches of the heavens, but not any more. If you want to know why, read my story.

Long ago, Owl sent messengers to the four corners of the world, calling all the birds to a meeting. Small as I am, I was happy to receive an invitation to this noble gathering, and I flew there in a great hurry.

Owl sat grandly in his old oak tree, his wise head slowly turning as he watched the horizon for his approaching guests. I was one of the first to arrive, and I perched close to him, wanting to be sure that I could hear his wise words.

Before long, the wide branches of his tree—then those of the neighboring trees as well—filled with the noisy racket of every kind of bird. There were gulls and geese, bluebirds and buzzards, cormorants and cuckoos, roadrunners and robins—every kind of bird you can imagine. Never before or since have so many birds gathered in one place. I was a little frightened by the numbers and the noise—but not too frightened, as you will see.

A single hoot from Owl brought silence to the crowd. Neither the rustle of a feather nor the click of a beak disturbed the hush that fell over the woods. "My friends," said Owl gravely, "I thank you all for coming."

He bowed to the flock, and a nervous murmur rolled over his listeners like a wave. All the birds were anxious to know the reason for this unusual assembly.

Owl turned his head and fixed his eyes intently upon the crowd. "We have a very grave problem. There is not one bird among us who will lead us in times of trouble, or rule and watch over us, or represent us in discussions with creatures that crawl upon the land or swim in the great waters. We have no one like the great bear or the mighty whale to stand before us. Even men and women have such leaders. It is my belief—and I hope you agree—that we, too, should have a leader, a king."

We were all silent at first, having no idea what to say, but a thought came to me: "It makes sense to have someone to represent the kingdom of birds."

"Why should we all of a sudden need a king?" asked Crow, the first to speak up. "We've never needed one before."

"What if we decide we don't like this new king?" asked Blue Jay.

"What if we don't want to do what this king says?" asked Osprey.

"How would we choose this king in the first place?" asked Robin.

Owl ignored all of the questions except the last one, to which he responded, "Ah-*hah*, a very important question, indeed!"

"Why don't you be king," asked Dove, "since you are wise and well liked?"

Owl put his head to one side and answered softly. "I am wise, it is true, but because I watch over the woods at night, I sleep all day. And you can't have a sleeping king!" He shook his head firmly. "No, no, it must be one of you."

One of us! My mind began to race, and before I knew it, the words spilled out of my foolish beak. "Which one of us? Do you mean any one of us?"

The other birds laughed and squawked rudely at me. Crane fell off his perch and landed flat on his back, stuck his long legs the air, and whooped and whooped until he began to cough.

Owl remained calm as he glared at rowdy Crane. Then he silenced the others with a wave of his wing. "Why shouldn't he or any one of you, large or small, be king? Do not mock! Wren, as small as he is, should have just as much of an opportunity to be king."

Another murmur arose, but it was Eagle who spoke up, asking, "Owl, tell us, how will we choose this king?"

Owl blinked his big orange eyes and said, "Well, I have an idea."

We listened closely, but I could hardly hear Owl above the pounding of my own heart. My mind was dizzy with the thought that even I might become king of the sky!

"We should hold a competition to see who can fly the highest," Owl said, "because in order to fly high, one must have courage, endurance, and the determination to keep on going upward, long after weaker birds have given up and come back to the ground. Courage, endurance, and determination—these are good qualities for a king!"

The birds all cheeped and squawked excitedly with one another, but my heart sank. How could I win a flying competition against bigger, stronger, more powerful creatures?

After several noisy minutes, the flock agreed that the high-flying competition would be held first thing in the morning.

The other birds all went to roost in nearby trees and fields, but not me. I had to work out a plan to try to win the competition.

Try as I might, I couldn't think of any possible way to win the contest on my own. I was simply too small and weak. I knew I couldn't fly as high as Osprey, Falcon, Hawk, or Eagle. I sat on a distant branch. Then, as I looked up at the stars in the nighttime sky, I began to wonder: "What if I could climb from point to point—from star to star, higher and higher into the sky? I could fly to the closest star and rest. Then I could continue on to the next star, and the next."

Of course, I couldn't possibly fly to even the nearest star, but the idea of flying part of the way, then resting, saving my strength until the end, got me thinking even more . . .

The next morning I moved close to the huddle of larger birds—Eagle, Falcon, Osprey, and Hawk.

"One of us will win," said Osprey, "since we are stronger than the others."

Eagle was not so sure, saying, "The others may travel higher because they are lighter."

While they were busy talking, I hopped up onto Eagle's back and hid in his long, brown feathers. He must have felt something, because he turned and scratched at his back with his huge beak. I don't know how he missed me!

Owl called all the birds to his oak tree for the start of the competition. At the drop of a feather, everyone soared high into the sky. I felt the steady flap of Eagle's great wings as he swept upward. I was terrified!

Higher and higher he went, rising through the clouds, and then, with a deep breath, he held his wings out wide and glided through the air, dipping and soaring.

Soon I knew I had come up with a good plan because the other birds began to fall behind. Eagle was indeed the master of the skies. I say *master*, not *king*, since I was going to be king!

As Eagle flew higher and higher, I could feel the beat of his heart, at first strong and rapid, but then, as the altitude increased, slower and weaker.

Eagle was tiring, and I knew he could not carry on much longer. I should have felt guilty about the extra load I was making him carry, but I did not. Finally, he started to sink a little, but as far as he knew, he had won the competition.

Now was my chance! I sprung from Eagle's broad back and danced into the sky, singing merrily as I climbed above his head, "King am I, King am I! Look at me, King of the Sky!"

I may be tiny, but I have a very big voice, and my tune carried through the air, down toward the astonished birds below.

As Eagle descended to the ground in defeat, I followed triumphantly, eager to see the other birds bow down before me. I could not wait for Owl to congratulate me on my brilliant plan, but—foolish me—I was to be disappointed.

Owl stared at me solemnly, unblinking and not speaking—but the others were hardly silent.

"Cheat!" called Crow.

"Trickster!" shouted Robin.

"What is this?" I thought, as a chorus of hisses and boos filled my ears. Had I not been clever and intelligent, and had I not outwitted them all?

Indeed I had, but none of them could accept my victory. All eyes were on Eagle, his head held low. He alone did not condemn me, but spoke softly to the flock.

"Wren has won, so now you must look to him, for he is your king." A tear sprang from Eagle's eye, and I knew I had not competed fairly.

Owl turned toward me and said sadly, "I must make an honest and fair judgment, because our choice of leader is most important."

He looked from me to Eagle and back again, and I knew what he would decide. He would say that I had cheated, and that I did not deserve to win. The mighty, noble Eagle would become our rightful king.

Indeed, those were his words. My pride turned to shame, my triumph to defeat.

So from that day to this, I have never risen above the level of the trees. You will never see me far from the ground. Only my voice goes high above the clouds. In the past, I went higher than Eagle, to the edge of the sky, but no more. Now you know why.

2
The Messenger: An Ethiopian Myth

The Weaver's Favorite

At the beginning of time, when everything was new, the great Weaver looked down upon his finest tapestry, the jungle, which was chock-full of life. Monkeys leaped from tree to tree, leopards lay on cool, mossy rocks, and hard-shelled tortoises eased through the undergrowth. All the creatures were happy in the jungle.

The Weaver was happy with all the jungle's creatures as well, but he liked one that walked on two legs in particular.

"What a fine being is Man," thought the Weaver. "So clever, so bright and full of energy. And all his shapes and sizes! Some are almost as tall as the giraffe, and others are as stocky as the rhinoceros, slender as the stork, or round as the hippo."

Then the Weaver looked more closely
into a clearing. In the village of Man,
youngsters played. The Weaver saw how
their arms and shoulders glowed in
the warm sun. The adults worked hard
gathering food and tending their homes.
Glistening droplets of sweat rolled over
their smooth, shiny skin. But the Weaver
paused as he saw the elders of the village,
whose skin had dried and wrinkled after
years in the jungle. The sun lay heavy on
their shoulders and weighed them down,
causing them to stoop and stumble.

"This will never do!" said the Weaver. "I
never intended for Man to have dried and
wrinkled skin. I already have the crocodile!

I want Man's skin to be smooth, soft, and beautiful to the end of his days."

The Weaver called his messenger bird to him. "Holawaka," he said, "I want you to take a message to one of the creatures in the jungle down below."

Holawaka settled on a nearby branch, ruffled his beautiful red-and-purple feathers, shook the golden comb on his head, and listened to his master, the Weaver.

"I will do as you say, Weaver," Holawaka squawked. "What is the message, and who is it for?"

"I want you to take a message to Man," said the Weaver. "Tell him to shed his skin when it starts to dry out and wrinkle, and show him how to wriggle out of it."

"Wriggle *out* of it?" squawked Holawaka with a flutter.

"Yes," replied the Weaver. "Underneath there will be new, soft skin."

Holawaka turned his head and pecked at an out-of-place feather. He plucked out the bent shaft and spat the feather to the ground, spluttering, "Why don't you just give Man feathers? It would save everyone a lot of time and effort. Everyone knows feathers are best!"

The Weaver shook his head and said, "Your feathers are quite nice, indeed, Holawaka, and they are perfect for you, but I hardly think they would suit Man. I want you to carry my message straight away, do you understand?"

Holawaka stretched lazily on his perch and muttered, "It seems like a silly message to me, but I will deliver it."

He stretched his wings as if to take flight, but then he hesitated and asked, "Weaver, what does this Man-being look like? You know all these common creatures look the same to me."

The Weaver glared angrily at the bird and said, "Holawaka, you are too unkind! Men and women are not common creatures. They are my favorites! You will do well to remember that!

"Man is easy to recognize. He walks upright and straight, his back shines like a jewel in the sun, and he moves with ease through the jungle. Go and find him before I decide to pluck your feathers for a fancy headdress!"

Flustered, Holawaka squawked and hopped off the branch. He launched himself into the air and extended his colorful wings to glide through the hot, humid canopy of the jungle, down toward the ground far below. The Weaver turned to other matters, trusting Holawaka to complete his task.

Once on the ground, Holawaka strutted importantly through the jungle, thinking, "I will deliver this message quickly, and then I will leave this awful jungle floor, where the twigs and stones hurt my delicate feet!"

As Holawaka tiptoed impatiently in the woody underbrush, the first creature that he met was Tortoise. Holawaka looked at his shiny, polished back. "Hmm," he thought. "I wonder if this is Man? His back certainly shines like a jewel in the sun."

Tortoise blinked at Holawaka twice and slowly opened his mouth as if to speak. But Holawaka shook his head and decided that this could not be Man, because Man moved swiftly through the jungle, and this creature was as slow as the sun when it traveled across the sky. Without even a polite nod to gentle Tortoise, Holawaka strutted on his way.

The next creature that he met was Leopard, sleek and silent, who moved swiftly through the jungle. Again Holawaka thought, "Perhaps this is Man," but when he looked more closely he saw that Leopard's back was covered with fur, not glistening skin, and that he walked close to the ground, not upright. No, this was not the creature that the Weaver had described. This was not the Weaver's favorite, Man.

Holawaka shook his head and moved on. He did not get a chance to speak to Leopard, for Leopard had already rushed off silently into the dark undergrowth.

Holawaka unfolded his wings and flapped them quickly, rising upward to a low-hanging limb. Coiled on the next tree branch was Snake. Holawaka had never seen Snake before, and the bird began to study the creature. Snake tested the air with his tongue. He raised his head high, lifting half the length of his body off the tree branch. Then Snake slid swiftly down the trunk and through the undergrowth, his skin sparkling in the light.

"That creature certainly moves quickly through the jungle, and upright, too," thought Holawaka, hopping a little closer. "Its slender back shines like the brightest jewel. Perhaps I have finally found Man. I must deliver my message!"

A short time later, Holawaka fluttered back into the top of the tallest tree, where he sat idly cleaning his feathers until the Weaver discovered that he had returned.

"Did you deliver my message?" the Weaver asked.

Holawaka answered importantly, "I have taken your message to Man."

The Weaver nodded his head with approval, saying, "Well done, my friend, and what exactly did you tell him?"

"I told him to shed his skin whenever it grew old and dry, and to wriggle out of it and leave it upon the ground to be carried away by the wind."

"And do you think he will?" asked the Weaver.

"Oh yes," replied Holawaka. "He assured me that he will do this regularly to keep his skin shiny and new."

This pleased the Weaver enormously, so he turned his mind to other matters. He trusted that Man would delight in his long-lasting beauty.

The Weaver was very busy, so by the time he next peered at the village of Man, the world was no longer a new place. All the creatures had gotten used to things, and their ways had become settled. The laws of nature had been made. It would have been difficult to unmake them.

The elders of the Man village still stooped and shuffled under the burden of the sun, and their skin had the dried, wrinkled look of old leather. And just there, at the base of a tall tree, the Weaver spotted Snake wriggling free of his old, dry skin, uncovering his glistening new back.

The Weaver sighed. He looked at Holawaka and shook his head. "I suppose I should have known better," the Weaver said. "If you want a job done well, you should do it yourself. Next time I'll deliver my own messages!"

And from that day to this, the Weaver always delivers his own messages, and Man always grows old and dry and wrinkly.

Holawaka, though, no longer has to play messenger. He has all the time in the world to clean his feathers.

Holawaka's Mistake
A Play

Cast of Characters

The Weaver

Holawaka

Tortoise

Leopard

Snake

SCENE 1:

Early morning in the jungle

Weaver: Holawaka, just look into the jungle down below. How fine are all the handsome creatures I have made!

Holawaka: Well, *you* might think so, but personally I'm not so sure.

Weaver: And why is that, Holawaka? What is wrong with them?

Holawaka: *(cleaning his feathers)* Not one of them has beautiful feathers like mine. They all have such common hides! Surely it would have been better to make more of them with feathers.

Weaver: *(shaking his head)* Ha, you foolish messenger bird. You need feathers to fly, but the creatures that roam the jungle floor do not need feathers. They need fur to keep them warm at night.

Holawaka: Perhaps . . . I can see that it keeps them warm, but I still don't think they're very handsome.

Weaver: Well I do, and I'm very pleased with all the creatures I've made—all but one. I'm having a little trouble with the upright one called Man.

Holawaka: What's the problem? I mean, apart from the fact that he doesn't have feathers, of course!

Weaver: *(sighing)* The problem is his skin, which is so beautiful when he is young. It is soft and smooth, and it shines like jewels in the warm sun, but as he grows old, it dries and wrinkles. It sags and droops. It must be very uncomfortable, and it spoils his beauty.

Holawaka: *(squawking)* So what are you going to do about it?

Weaver: *(sadly)* I'm not sure what I *can* do. Do you have a suggestion?

Holawaka: *(tugging at a feather)* Well, when my feathers get old and tattered, I shed them. My feathers drop off, and I grow new ones in their place.

Weaver: What a fantastic idea! Man could shed his old skin and grow a new one in its place! Since you are my messenger bird, I want you to go straight down and tell Man that when he starts to wrinkle, if he wriggles out of his old skin, he will find a new one in its place.

Holawaka: *(squawking)* Fine, but remind me again what this Man looks like. All those sorry ground creatures appear the same to me.

Weaver: Holawaka, the only creature you ever notice is yourself! Now listen carefully. Man stands upright. He is agile and moves quickly through the jungle. Most importantly, his skin is smooth and shiny. Now, off you go, and I'll see you later. I have work to do.

SCENE 2:

On the jungle floor

Holawaka: Aargh, all these twigs hurt my toes! I don't like it down here on the floor of the jungle. I hope I can find Man soon so that I can give him this message. Then I'll get out of here! Oh, is this Man coming towards me now?

Tortoise: *(moving and talking very slowly)* Hello . . . strange . . . bird. How . . . are . . . you . . . today?

Holawaka: I'm fine, apart from my poor feet, but just let me take a look at you. You have such a lovely, polished back, so shiny—like a jewel! I guess you must be Man! What a piece of luck to find you so soon.

Tortoise: Who . . . ? Me . . . ? Man . . . ?

Holawaka: Well, you fit the Weaver's description—but wait, Man travels swiftly through the jungle. Hmm . . . you're not exactly swift, are you? And you don't appear to stand upright.

Tortoise: I'm . . . very . . . swift . . . ! Watch . . . me . . . go . . . !

Holawaka: *(interrupting)* Um, you know, I don't have all day. You can't possibly be Man.

(Holawaka moves on.)

Holawaka: Ah now, who is that moving swiftly through the brush? Is that Man? Excuse me, please! Stop, I want a word with you!

Leopard: Who, me?

Holawaka: Yes, you. You are sleek and swift, and I see how easily you move. I think I have a message for you. Come closer so I may see you better.

Leopard: *(pouncing)* Is that close enough?

Holawaka: *(fluttering up into a tree)* Too close! I said I wanted to see you, not feel your claws! Keep your distance now, thank you very much!

Leopard: Hmmm, yes, feathers. Nasty things—spoil one's lunch.

Holawaka: Nasty? They aren't nasty! They're beautiful—much more beautiful than your dull yellow fur . . . wait! Yellow fur? That's not right—Man doesn't have fur!

Leopard: Of course he doesn't. I do, so stop wasting my time and give me the message before I ignore the feathers and have you for lunch anyway!

Holawaka: I don't think so! And besides, the message isn't for you! *(Holawaka flutters into the air as Leopard lunges toward the bird.)*

Holawaka: Whew! That was close! Now I must find Man—and quickly, because I have to get out of this dangerous jungle! Ah, just my luck—that might be him now!

Snake: *(slithering through the undergrowth)* Hissss. Out of my way, bird! I'm in a hurry.

Holawaka: Slow down, my friend! You're just the creature I've been looking for.

Snake: Well, you're not the creature *I've* been looking for, so just stay out of my way—unless, of course, you fancy being . . . uh, I mean, *having* lunch.

Holawaka: *(squawking in alarm)* Ah, no, thank you! I just escaped being . . . I mean, it's past my lunchtime.

Snake: Are you *sure?*

Holawaka: Oh yes! But I have been looking for you all morning. I've been seeking someone who moves quickly—that appears to be you. I've been looking for someone with skin that shines like jewels—that's you. Ah, but I'm also seeking someone who stands upright, and . . . well . . .

Snake: *(rises up)* Do you mean like this?

Holawaka: Yes! Yes! That's it! Oh, you must be Man! I have an important message for you from the great Weaver!

Snake: Man, eh? *Weaver,* eh? Go on, then. I'm listening.

Holawaka: Well, the Weaver says . . .

SCENE 3:

Back in the jungle canopy

Weaver: Oh, there you are, Holawaka. You were gone a long time. Did you find Man and give him my message?

Holawaka: *(squawking)* I certainly was gone a long time—far too long—and yes, I did deliver your message.

Weaver: Did you explain how to wriggle out of his skin when it became old and wrinkled?

Holawaka: Yes, I did.

Weaver: And did you tell him about the smooth and shiny new skin he'd find underneath?

Holawaka: Yes, I did. Look, there he goes now, showing off his new skin to everyone. Doesn't he look handsome!

Weaver: What? Where? *There?* Slipping through the jungle on his belly? That's not Man! That is Snake! Oh, Holawaka, what have you done?

Holawaka: Uh, well . . .

Weaver: Man spends his days in the warm sun, working harder than ever. He grows ever older and more wrinkled. And Snake—*Snake*, of all the creatures on Earth!—slips around the jungle in brand new skin.

Holawaka: Oh, dear. What are you going to do about it?

Weaver: Do about it? What *can* I do about it? Snake is able to shed his skin, and Man must live out his years in a wrinkled old hide.

Holawaka: So you'll just leave things as they are?

Weaver: Oh, Holawaka, what a most troublesome bird you are! Get out of my sight before I turn you into a feather duster.

Holawaka: All right, but I told you that you should have simply given Man feathers in the first place.

3
The Phoenix Myths

In the heat of the desert, a small bird tries to build its nest. It cannot make a nest on the sandy desert floor, for the heat would cook its eggs long before they hatched. It cannot make its nest in the branches of a tree, for there are no trees in this arid land. So the clever bird builds a mound. Higher and higher, the mound rises from the desert floor until, on the top, the brave bird builds its nest, far enough from the ground to be safe. As the bird sits on its nest, the heat of the desert rises and ripples around it, making the nest look as if it is being engulfed in flames. Perhaps this is the origin of the legend of the Phoenix—a legend told in many different cultures. Here are two versions of the myth, one from Egypt and the other from Greece.

The Golden Phoenix of Egypt

In the hour before dawn, all was silent.
The sun lay hidden behind distant hills.
The world held its breath, waiting for the
moment when the first bright rays would
chase away the darkness of the night.

Suddenly, a piercing cry was heard. It
was Ra, lord of the sun, calling for the
Phoenix to fly from the distant East and
bring with him the sun's golden globe.

The Phoenix rose up from the dark
blanket of the night. It streaked across the
sky, streamers of fire trailing behind it.
Clinging to these bright streamers was the
burning sun.

Ra watched with pride as the Phoenix climbed into the sky. Without the gift of the sun, the world would always remain wrapped in cold and darkness. The earth would not be able to bring forth flowers, fruit, or crops to feed its countless creatures. Ra's flaming gift was indeed an important one.

The Phoenix settled at the feet of Ra and said, "I have started the sun on its journey."

"You've done well, Phoenix," Ra answered. "Go now and spend your day relaxing until we meet again this evening."

The Phoenix turned to go, but Ra held him back for a moment and said, "I know that your time is running out, but do not let your rest cause you to forget your duty. The whole world relies upon you to cover it with night's blanket later."

The Phoenix bowed his head, his white-feathered crest almost touching the baking-hot sand. He never forgot his duty. He was never late.

Every morning, for five hundred years, he had brought the sun from the East to light the morning, and every evening for just as long, he had guided the sun back to its resting place behind the distant hills, so the world could once again sleep in cool darkness. But a time of change was approaching.

The Phoenix flapped his wings and flew off toward the temple of the sun. There he perched upon a sacred stone and warmed his feathers in the yellow glow of the morning. In the bright sunlight, the Phoenix's chest shone scarlet, his wings golden, and his feathered crest a pure, gleaming white.

It was rare to see the Phoenix at the temple. People stopped what they were doing and looked through the narrow windows to stare at the strange beauty of the bird. How could one work or eat or go about one's business when the beautiful Phoenix was present? It was nearly impossible, since the Phoenix was such a remarkable thing to see.

Today, though, the bird visited the temple because he had a special task to perform. For hundreds of years, he had carried the sun through the sky, morning and evening, without complaining. But lately he had begun to grow tired. He didn't die, like any other sort of bird. The Phoenix had a special way of renewing himself—of being reborn—so that he could regain his strength and youth. Tomorrow the time for such renewal would come. Only one more evening would pass before he could change again into his youthful form.

After he rested, the Phoenix flew to a large willow tree that stood in a garden near the grounds of the temple. Here he would build a nest. But he wouldn't build it from common twigs or grass. Instead, the Phoenix would construct the nest from the branches of the sweetest-smelling plants, shrubs, and trees that he could find.

All afternoon long he flew back and forth, gathering his special perfumed materials—cinnamon bark, rose stems, honeysuckle, and jasmine. The Phoenix skillfully weaved the stems and strands together, until their scents filled the garden, and a large and beautiful nest took shape.

At last his task was completed, and the Phoenix stood back and looked at his nest. He was satisfied that the beautiful nest would serve its purpose well. Only one more task needed to be finished before he could begin his process of rebirth.

The day was growing old. The earth and its creatures had become weary from the heat and looked for shelter from the sun's punishing rays. The Phoenix took one more look at his nest, and then he flew back over the desert, rising higher and higher into the sky toward the burning sun.

As the Phoenix approached the giant ball of flame, Ra met him and said, "You have done well, my golden bird. Your nest is prepared. After you guide the sun back to its resting place tonight, you can begin your renewal."

The Phoenix flew around the sun, his crimson-and-gold feathers glowing in the heat. He caught the reins of the sun in his beak and tugged the huge sphere downward toward the far horizon. Lower and lower the sun sank, until only a thin orange rim could be seen peeking above the distant hills.

The sky turned a deep purple, and then blackness descended. The calm of the night lay all around, and the Phoenix's job was finished. He beat his wings and flew quietly back across the desert to the city of the sun. All was silent there as well. He circled above the temple once, and then landed upon his flowered nest. He made himself comfortable, breathed in the sweet scents surrounding him, and very soon had fallen fast asleep.

The next day, the world waited for the familiar call for the sun, but no one heard a sound. Instead, just before the time when dawn should have brightened the morning skies, Ra visited the Phoenix at his flowery nest. He gazed on the sleeping bird before waking him.

"It is time," Ra said. He reached out and lifted the sun into the morning sky. Ra positioned the sun closer and closer to the Phoenix's nest, until tiny wisps of smoke began to curl from the scented stems. A strong perfume filled the air as the nest became hotter and hotter, and then, with a sudden spark, the nest caught fire.

Before Ra's eyes the Phoenix burned down to nothing but a small pile of ashes. But rather than be saddened by the loss of the bird, Ra smiled, for this was a moment of rebirth. As the nest cooled, a tiny, downy bird pushed its head up through the mound of grey ashes and looked skyward. The warm rays of the sun shone down on him and soothed the little creature.

"Welcome back!" said Ra brightly.

The Phoenix struggled to one side of the nest, gathered his strength, and beat his tiny wings. A cloud of grey dust rose around him.

"You must gather up the ashes," said Ra, "and lay them on the sacred stone in the temple of the sun. Then you may fly to the East and rest until morning."

The tiny Phoenix obeyed Ra's command and gathered the ashes together in a pile. But how was he to carry them? He tried his best to remember how he had collected the ashes before—five hundred years ago—and when the memory came to him, he got to work.

The Phoenix gathered together a ball of scented sap from a nearby tree and shaped it into an egg. He pecked a hole in the center and filled it with the grey ashes of his old self. Then he sealed the hole with more sap. The Phoenix carried the ash-filled egg to the temple and gently placed it upon the sacred stone. His task was done.

Ra hid the sun behind the distant hills that night, but the next morning, just before dawn, the familiar cry was heard once again. At Ra's request, the golden Phoenix, now rested, youthful, and strong, rose into the gloomy darkness and streaked across the sky. Fiery streamers trailed behind him, and clinging to these streamers was Ra's great gift. The sun appeared once again to wake the sleeping world.

The Crimson Phoenix of Greece

The early-morning sky was dusted with orange, pink, and blue. In the highest branches of a twisted old tree, Phoenix, a most beautiful creature, awoke. He opened his golden beak wide with a huge yawn, and he gently flapped his red-and-purple wings to chase the stiffness from them.

Phoenix was an old bird. His wings and his legs, and sometimes even his beak, were stiff and sore when he woke in the morning. He knew it was time to wake up because the morning light was gently peeking across the desert from the far horizon. Slowly, he hopped off his perch and fluttered down to drink from the well that nestled in a stand of palm trees.

He swallowed the cool water, which was made sweet by the dates that had fallen from the shading palms. Phoenix then turned his head skyward and sang out. His voice was clear and mellow, like a single note from a flute.

His melody swirled into the well, echoing from the walls. Then it rose upward and poured out over the still desert morning like a soft breeze.

Everything else was silent. It was as if the whole world had stopped to listen to this remarkable sound. Even the sun lord, Apollo, in his daily journey across the sky, stopped his chariot long enough to listen for a while.

"Who is making that beautiful music?" asked Apollo.

No answer came, for all the creatures in the desert were themselves busy listening to Phoenix's voice.

Apollo had stopped his chariot, and the sun paused in the sky, and the morning got no later. The sun wouldn't move until Apollo knew who or what was singing.

Phoenix took off and flew upward, eventually landing on Apollo's shoulder. Now he sang directly into Apollo's ear.

"Ah, Phoenix," sighed Apollo, "I should have guessed that your voice would match the beauty of your lovely feathers. May both live forever, like you."

"Phoenix cannot live forever," interrupted the burning voice of the sun. "He lives for only five hundred years—no more."

"Five hundred years?" wondered Apollo. "And just how long has he lived so far?"

Not even the sun knew the answer to this question, and Apollo grew very troubled. The sun lord turned to Phoenix and spoke in a determined voice, "From this day forward, every morning when I guide my chariot across the sky, driving the burning sun through its daily course, I will stop for a moment or two and listen to your song." Then he added, more gently, "But I do not wish to stop one morning and find that you are no longer singing. That won't do at all!"

He thought to himself for a moment, and then he motioned for the Phoenix to come closer, saying, "Listen carefully, and I will tell you what you must do when your five hundred years are almost over."

Apollo then whispered into Phoenix's ear. Phoenix listened and committed the sun lord's words to memory. From that day on, he sang his thanks to Apollo each morning as the sun rose and every evening as the sun set.

Several years passed, and Phoenix grew in beauty. His voice was said to be made of pure gold, and his lovely feathers were thought to have remarkable powers. For instance, if they dropped out and fell to the ground as Phoenix flew over the desert, creatures would collect them and use them to cure sickness and disease. Phoenix needed no food. He lived on air and water alone, for he refused to bring harm to any creature—or indeed any living thing, plant or animal. When he cried tears, droplets of the finest perfume fell from his eyes.

As the end of his five hundred years grew near, Phoenix thought of Apollo's words and began his preparations. From tree to tree he gathered sweet-smelling branches, blossoms, spices, nectar, and fruit. Then he found the tallest palm tree in the entire desert. There, with the care of an artist, he skillfully wove a mat on which to rest.

When the sun rose the next morning, Phoenix started to sing, but the only drink he had with which to ease his thirst was the drops of dew that had collected on the edge of the mat.

Apollo flew by with his chariot and horses, towing the sun to the top of the sky. He asked the Phoenix, "You're not at the well today?"

Apollo followed Phoenix's gaze as the bird turned his beautiful head and looked towards the west, to the land of the setting sun.

"Ah," Apollo said. "I understand." Then Apollo caught a scent in the air. He spied the sweet-smelling mat where Phoenix was perched.

"You remembered!" Apollo cried. With a smile, he pulled on the reins. The horses reared up, snorting loudly, and as their legs waved in the air, sparks shot from their hooves and dropped onto Phoenix's mat.

Almost at once, a dense smoke filled the air. The mat began to burn gently, and then, with a roar, it erupted into brilliant flames.

Phoenix turned his head to the morning sky and sang in his strongest, clearest voice. When the flames died down, there was only silence.

Days passed, and no song greeted the dawn. Apollo steered his chariot upward and looked neither right nor left. But on the ninth day, something caught the sun lord's eye. He stopped near the palm tree and peered at the remains of Phoenix's mat. There, among the cold grey ashes, sat a tiny bird.

"There you are!" boomed Apollo, and the little bird lifted his head and tried to sing. "Hush," urged Apollo. "Save your strength. You have an important job to do."

The little bird cocked his head, and fixed his beady eyes on the far horizon. "That's right," said Apollo, "but take your time. Go slowly at first."

And that is what the little bird did. Phoenix took his time preparing for the solemn task of carrying the cold grey ashes to their final place of rest. Every day he flexed his wings, gaining strength and power, and when he was strong enough to leave the nest, he practiced carrying small items, such as twigs and pebbles, in his beak.

At last, the important day arrived. Young Phoenix lifted the blackened remains of the mat, flew strongly all the way to the sacred resting place, and there, on a stone bathed by the sun, he laid his burden of ashes.

His task complete, he flew eastward, back across the desert, to the land of the rising sun. And there, beside a well shaded by tall palms and sweetened by fallen dates, Phoenix drank his fill. He needed his voice to be strong and clear at sunrise.